LUKE T]

C000126203

Rhinoceros:
The Haunting of Ganda

BROKEN SLEEP BOOKS

Published 2020,
Broken Sleep Books:
Cornwall / Wales

brokensleepbooks.com

First Edition

Lay out your unrest.

Illustration: CF Sherratt
Publisher/Editor: Aaron Kent
Editor: Charlie Baylis

Typeset in UK by Aaron Kent

Broken Sleep Books is committed to
a sustainable future for our planet,
and therefore uses print on
demand publication.

ISBN: 978-1-913642-20-4

Contents

If one does not understand the usefulness of the useless and the uselessness of the useful, one cannot understand art.

- Eugene Ionesco
- translated by Thomas Merton

Rhinoceros:
The Haunting of Ganda

Luke Thompson

with rhino illustrations by:
CF Sherratt

Introduction

Ganda is the most talked about rhinoceros in the history of rhinoceroses. He (other writers have referred to Ganda as a 'he', which we'll assume is correct, although the only image of Ganda alongside a human – a detail of a 1515 or 1517 work by Francesco Granacci – suggests a smaller, possibly female, rhinoceros. There are two uncertainties with this idea: firstly, we do not know the height of the person standing alongside Ganda; and secondly, the painting was done after Ganda had died, so might have been, to some extent, from memory or from earlier sketches) has had a BBC Radio 4 programme and a long novel written about him, as well as numerous chapters in books on art history, sketches, engravings, paintings, postcards, essays…

At the root of this interest is a single woodcut by the celebrated German artist Albrecht Dürer, a copy of which is kept at the British Museum. The woodcut was made following the sensational arrival of the first Indian rhinoceros to appear in Europe since Roman times, who landed in Lisbon in 1515. The rhinoceros was named Ganda.

Dürer's image is remarkable, influenced by contemporary texts as well as texts by natural historians and writers of bestiaries through the ages. The rhinoceros, monoceros, or unicorn, was a mythic species, yet here it was in the age of economic and colonial expansion in Europe – the age of the High Renaissance in art – the age of Leonardo da Vinci, Copernicus, John Locke, Hieronymus Bosch, Machiavelli and the Medicis, as well as of Cornelius Agrippa, Paracelsus and Faust.

...

Ganda was a political gift, captured, chained and shipped from India to Portugal along the new trade route. In Europe, Ganda represented the Indian rhinoceros as a species – he was their only example – and it is as an example of the species that he was treated. This is where my interest began.

...

Natural history has not always been great at looking at individual animals. We tend to be interested in how dolphins-as-such behave, or hippopotamuses-as-such, or robins-as-such, or otters-as-such, and not how *this* robin behaves, or *this* dolphin. When Stephen Moss published his recent books about robins and wrens he named them *The Robin: A Biography* and *The Wren: A Biography*, the titles implying that there is only one life for the total of each species.[1]

This is not the case with people. We have been interested in individuals throughout literary history, from Plutarch's *Lives* of legendary heroes and Suetonius's *Lives of the Caesars*, through the early medieval hagiographies, Vasari's *Lives of the Artists*, Aubrey's *Brief Lives*, and to the contemporary bestselling genres of biography, autobiography and memoir, which include stories of surgeons and sports people and lighthouse keepers and human rights

---

1   In the books themselves Moss does not suggest this at all. It is only the titles being critiqued here, and these are quite likely to have been chosen for their marketability, animal lives having become a bit of a thing.

campaigners and people who have recovered from illnesses and singers and reality TV stars and chefs.

…

Elephants have a handful of champions within the field of ethnoelephantology arguing for elephants to be considered as individuals rather than each being considered to have identical needs, but the human-elephant relationship has a different cultural history from the human-rhinoceros. Look at Babar and look at Rataxes.

…

The rhinoceros is a charismatic but misused species. It is big, powerful and looks aggressive with its squat, muscular form, armoured cladding and prominent horn. It is easy to anthropomorphise, to caricature, and historically, in literature and film, it has been represented as a stupid, slow and violent animal. It is one of the baddies, an antagonist, a brute.

…

There is a missing scene from Disney's 1967 *The Jungle Book*, which was written and storyboarded but never animated. Mowgli is tricked by the vultures into climbing a boulder to look for Rocky. Only it wasn't a boulder, it was the sleeping rhinoceros himself, who is woken and keen to fight. Rocky is a dim and short-sighted creature and he charges at Mowgli, guided by the vultures, until Mowgli leaps out of the way and Rocky hits a real boulder, bending his horn. Mowgli is declared the winner of the fight and they all sing a song about friendship.[2] [3]

...

Even Ganda's name is suggestive of the generic, being derived from the Gujarati for 'rhinoceros'. They named their rhinoceros *rhinoceros*.

...

In this sequence on Ganda I am playing with ideas of who Ganda was or might have been and where he fits within perceptions of the rhinoceros-as-such, what the rhinoceros-as-such has meant and what this rhinoceros in particular might mean. The meandering mosaic of this text might deviate in any number of ways from the central subject, exploring seams and themes. Abstraction, identity, presence, the body and isolation all naturally emerge and submerge in the folds of the text(s).

...

---

[2]   Trivia: Rocky was to be voiced by Frank Fontaine, who was making a career from playing comic idiots and drunks.

[3]   Extra trivia: Disney often uses characters multiple times, almost like real actors. Bill the Lizard from *Alice in Wonderland*, for instance, also appears in *The Great Mouse Detective* as one of Ratigan's goons. Similarly, Rocky appears briefly in *Bedknobs and Broomsticks*, in the crowd of the cartoon football match, just to the right (our left) of the royal box.

As the sole representative of Indian rhinos in Europe at the time, Ganda drew to him all of the European literature written about the rhinoceros, monoceros and unicorn. People looked for the historic qualities in Ganda, and their responses to him were coloured by the literary context.

...

I picture the history of Ganda as an hourglass tipped on its side. Ganda is the central point at which the two triangles meet. To the left of Ganda is the past, a massive unruly history of European speculation about what a rhinoceros, monoceros or unicorn looks like, how it behaves, what it means. This mass is at no point informed by experience. None of the historians, natural historians, travellers, pseudo-travellers or theologians saw one. Then Ganda arrives in Portugal, that small single point in the centre. A real rhinoceros, a seemingly docile monster, an opportunity to rectify the myths. Still, there are few surviving accounts of Ganda from those who saw him themselves. The right-hand triangle is post-Ganda Europe, a history once again full of stories of the rhinoceros – etchings, drawings, poems – and once again none of them were drawn from life. Dürer did not see Ganda, and neither did any of the myriad writers and artists copying his artwork.

The Ganda we receive is a Ganda of fragments, allusions, grotesques and ghosts.

The Prehistory of Ganda

The Bible

The Bible is full of unicorns. Sort of. That is, the Biblical Hebrew *re'em* was translated into the Greek *monoceros*, which was then translated into the Latin *unicornus*, which was then translated into the English *unicorn*. And so we find English Bible translations packed with unicorns. There is lots of lovely debate about whether this is really a rhinoceros, an auroch, a kind of ox or something else altogether, and different Bibles translate the word in all sorts of ways.

Numbers 24:8

God brought him forth out of Egypt; he hath as it were the strength of an unicorn: he shall eat up the nations his enemies, and shall break their bones, and pierce them through with his arrows.

Deuteronomy 33:17

His glory is like the firstling of his bullock, and his horns are like the horns of unicorns: with them he shall push the people together to the ends of the earth: and they are the ten thousands of Ephraim, and they are the thousands of Manasseh.

Job 39:9-10

Will the unicorn be willing to serve thee, or abide by thy crib?
Canst thou bind the unicorn with his band in the furrow? or will he harrow the valleys after thee?

Psalm 92:10

But my horn shalt thou exalt like the horn of an unicorn

ʿ

Diodorus (1st Century BCE)
The Library of History
(CH Oldfather translation, published by Loeb Classical Library, 1935)

At the tip of its nostrils it carries a horn which may be described as snub and in hardness is like iron. Since it is ever contesting with the elephant about pasturage it sharpens its horn on stones, and when it opens the fight with this animal it slips under its belly and rips open the flesh with its horn as with a sword. By adopting this kind of fighting it drains the blood of the beasts and kills many of them. But if the elephant has avoided the attempt of the rhinoceros to get under his belly and has seized it beforehand with his trunk, he easily overcomes it by goring it with its tusks and making use of its superior strength.

Martial (C.38-104AD)[4]
Epigrams

(Henry George Bohn translation, published by G. Bell and sons, 1897.)

On the Rhinoceros

The rhinoceros exhibited for thee, Caesar, in the whole space of the arena, fought battles of which he gave no promise. Oh, into what terrible wrath did he with lowered head blaze forth! How powerful was that tusk to whom a bull was a mere ball!

> He who with armed nostril wildly glared,
> Has fought the battles he had not declared.
> How did his headlong rage the pit appal!
> How flash'd the horn that made a bull a ball!

Elphinston

---

4   Martial was a first century Roman poet, known for his vast collection of 'epigrams'. Epigrams were an ancient Greek and Roman poetic genre, and Martial was a master of them, each short poem ending with a witticism or punchline.

In the translation favoured here, Henry George Bohn has first rendered the original text in prose and then paired it up with a poetic version by an English poet. Whenever they couldn't find a better poet, Bohn explains in his introduction, he hopes the reader will forgive him for having used the 'indifferent' poet Elphinston's verse. Elphinston's poetic translations of Martial were so bad that in an idle moment Robert Burns even mocked them:

> O thou whom Poesy abhors,
> Whom Prose has turned out of doors!
> Heard'st thou yon groan? Proceed no further;
> 'Twas laurell'd Martial calling Murther!

Happily, all of the sections of Martial relating to the rhinoceros have Elphinston's murderous versionings.

On a Rhinoceros

While the trembling keepers were exciting the rhinoceros, and the wrath of the huge animal had been long arousing itself, the conflicts of the promised engagement were beginning to be despaired of; but at length his fury, well-known of old, returned. For easily as a bull tosses to the skies the balls placed upon *his horns*, so with his double horn did he hurl aloft the heavy bear.

> While long they roused the hero to engage,
> And bid his nostrils gather all their rage,
> In vain the timid guides for battle burn'd;
> When lo! the glory of his power return'd:
> High a huge bear he heaved with double horn,
> As a bull sends aloft the balls that brave his scorn.

Elphinston

Pliny the Elder (23-79AD)
Natural History
(Philemon Holland translation, 1601)

8:20

In the same Plays of Pompey, and many Times beside was shewed a Rhinoceros, with a single Horn on his Snout. This is a second begotten Enemy to the Elephant. He fileth this Horn against hard Stones, and so prepareth himself to fight; and in his Conflict he aimeth principally at the Belly, which he knoweth to be the tenderest Part. He is full as long as his enemy; his Legs much shorter; his Colour a palish Yellow.

8:21

But the most furious Beast is the Monoceros: his Body resembleth an Horse, his Head a Stag, his Feet an Elephant, his Tail a Boar; the Sound he utters is deep; there is one black Horn in the Middle of his Forehead, projecting two Cubits in Length: by Report, this Wild Beast cannot possibly be caught alive.

Ctesias (C.5TH BC), Photios (C.810-893AD) And Aelian (C.175-235AD)
India

(The *India* of Ctesias is a lost text, parts of which are preserved in fragments of the work of Photios and Aelian (amongst others) translated here by J.W. McCrindle in *Ancient India as Described by Ktêsias the Knidian*, published by Trübner & Co, 1882.)

Photios

Among the Indians, he [Ctesias] proceeds, there are wild asses as large as horses, some being even larger. Their head is of a dark red colour, their eyes blue, and the rest of their body white. They have a horn on their forehead, a cubit in length [the filings of this horn, if given in a potion, are an antidote to poisonous drugs]. This horn for about two palm-breadths upwards from the base is of the purest white, where it tapers to a sharp point of a flaming crimson, and, in the middle, is black. These horns are made into drinking cups, and such as drink from them are attacked neither by convulsions nor by the sacred disease (epilepsy). Nay, they are not even affected by poisons, if either before or after swallowing them they drink from these cups wine, water, or anything else. While other asses moreover, whether wild or tame, and indeed all other solid-hoofed animals have neither huckle-bones, nor gall in the liver, these one-horned asses have both. Their huckle-bone is the most beautiful of all I have ever seen, and is, in appearance and size, like that of the ox. It is as heavy as lead, and of the colour of cinnabar both on the surface, and all throughout. It is exceedingly fleet and strong, and no creature that pursues it, not even the horse, can overtake it.

On first starting it scampers off somewhat leisurely, but the longer it runs, it gallops faster and faster till the pace becomes most furious. These animals therefore can only be caught at one particular time — that is when they lead out their little foals to the pastures in which they roam. They are then hemmed in on all sides by a vast number of hunters mounted on horseback, and being unwilling to escape while leaving their young to perish, stand their ground and fight, and by butting with their horns and kicking and biting kill many horses and men. But they are in the end taken, pierced to death with arrows and spears, for to take them alive is in no way possible. Their flesh being bitter is unfit for food, and they are hunted merely for the sake of their horns and their huckle-bones.

Aelian

I have ascertained by enquiry that wild asses are found in India as big as horses. The animal is entirely white, except about the head, which is of a reddish colour, while the eye gleams with azure. It has a horn upon its forehead about a cubit and a half long. This horn is white at the base, crimson at the tip, and jet black in the middle. These particoloured horns are used, I understand, as drinking cups by the Indians, not indeed by people of all ranks, but only by the magnates, who rim them at intervals with circlets of gold just as they would adorn with bracelets the arm of some beautiful statue. They say that whoever drinks out of this horn is protected against all incurable diseases, for he can neither be seized by convulsions nor by what is called the sacred disease (epilepsy), and neither can he be cut off by poison; nay if before drinking from it he should have swallowed anything deleterious, he vomits this, and escapes scatheless from all ill effects, and while, as has been believed, all other asses, wherever found, and whether wild or tame, and even all solid-hoofed animals, have neither a huckle-bone nor a gall in the liver, the Indian horned asses have according to Ktesias both a huckle-bone and a gall in the liver. The huckle-bones are said to be black, not only on the surface but all throughout as may be proved by breaking one to pieces. They are fleeter not only than other asses but even than horses and deer. On first starting they run leisurely, but they gradually strengthen their pace, and then to overtake them, is, to use a poetic expression, the unattainable. When the dams have brought forth and begin to lead out their young ones to the pastures, the males are in close attendance, and guard their offspring with devoted care. They roam about in the most desolate tracts of the Indian plain, and when the hunters come to attack them, they relegate their foals, being as yet but young and tender, to graze in the rear, while in front they fight to defend them. Their mode of attack is to charge the horsemen, using the horn as the weapon of assault, and this is so powerful, that nothing can withstand the blow it gives, but yields and snaps in two, or is perhaps shivered to pieces and spoiled for further use. They sometimes even fall upon the horses, and so cruelly rip up their sides with the horn that their very entrails gush out. The riders, it may well be imagined, dread to encounter them at close quarters, since the penalty of approaching them is a miserable death both to man and horse. And not only do they butt, but they also kick most viciously and bite ; and their bite is much to be dreaded, for they tear away all the flesh they grasp with their teeth. It is accordingly impossible to take them alive if they be full-grown; and hence they must be despatched with such missiles as the spear or the arrow. This done, the Indians despoil them of their horns, which they ornament in the manner already described. The flesh is so very bitter that the Indians cannot use it for food.

Aelian (C.175-235AD)
On the Nature of Animals
(Translated by AF Scholfield, Loeb Classical Library, 1958)

India produces horses with one horn, they say, and the same country fosters asses with a single horn. And from these horns they make drinking-vessels, and if anyone puts a deadly poison in them and a man drinks, the plot will do him no harm. For it seems that the horn both of the horse and of the ass is an antidote to the poison.

St Basil (329-379)
Exegetic Homilies

(*Translated by Sister Agnes Clare Way, published by The Catholic University of America Press, 1953*)

But, when it is necessary to take vengeance and to overthrow the power attacking the race of men, a certain wild and savage force, then He will be called the Son of unicorns. For, as we have learned in Job, the unicorn is a creature, irresistible in might and unsubjected to man. 'For, thou canst not bind him with a thong,' he says, 'nor will he stay at thy crib.' There is also much said in that part of the prophecy about the animal acting like a free man and not submitting to men. It has been observed that the Scripture has used the comparison of the unicorn in both ways, at one time in praise, at another in censure. 'Deliver,' he says, 'my soul from the sword . . . and my lowness from the horns of the unicorns.' He said these words complaining of the warlike people who in the time of passion rose up in rebellion against him. Again, he says, 'My horn shall be exalted like that of the unicorn.' It seems that on account of the promptness of the animal in repelling attacks it is frequently found representing the baser things, and because of its high horn and freedom it is assigned to represent the better. On the whole, since it is possible to find the 'horn' used by Scripture in many places instead of 'glory', as the saying: 'He will exalt the horn of his people,' and 'His horn shall be exalted in glory,' or also, since the 'horn' is frequently used instead of 'power,' as the saying: 'My protector and the horn of my salvation,' Christ is the power of God; therefore, He is called the Unicorn on the ground that He has one horn, that is, one common power with the Father.

Kosmas Indikopleustes (6th Century) De Mundo

(Translated by J.W. McCrindle as an appendix in Ancient India as Described by Ktêsias the Knidian, published by Trübner & Co, 1882)

The Rhinoceros

This animal is called the rhinoceros from having horns growing upon its nose. When it walks about the horns shake, but when it looks enraged it tightens them, and they become firm and unshaken so that they are able to tear up even trees by the roots, such especially as stand in their way. The eyes are placed as low down as the jaws. It is altogether a most terrible animal, and is especially hostile to the elephant. Its feet and its skin closely resemble those of the elephant. Its skin, which is dry and hard, is four fingers thick – and from this instead of from iron some make ploughshares wherewith they plough their lands. The Ethiopians in their language call the rhinoceros *arou* or *harisi*, prefixing the rough breathing to the *alpha* of the word, and adding *risi* to it, so that the word *arou* is the name of the animal, while *harisi* is an epithet which indicates its connexion with *ploughing* arising from the configuration of its nose and the use made of its hide. I have seen a living rhinoceros, but I was standing some distance off at the time. I have also seen the skin of one, which was stuffed with straw and stood in the king's palace, and I have thus been enabled to delineate the animal accurately.

The Monokeros or Unicorn

This animal is called the unicorn, but I have never set eyes upon it. I have however seen *four* brazen statues of it in Ethiopia, where they were set up in the royal palace – an edifice adorned with four towers. From these statues I have thus delineated the animal. They say of it that it is a terrible beast and invincible, having its power all lodged in its horn. When it perceives that its pursuers are many and that they are on the point of catching it, it springs down from the top of some precipice, and during the descent through the air turns itself in such a way that the whole shock of the fall is sustained by the horn which receives no damage thereby. [...]

Isidore of Seville (C.560-636)
Etymologies

(translated by Stephen A. Barney, W.J. Lewis, J.A. Beach and Oliver Berghof, published by Cambridge University Press, 2006)

The rhinoceros (*rhinoceron*) is named with a Greek word; in Latin it means 'horn on the nose.' This is also the *monoceron*, that is, the unicorn (*unicornus*), because it has a single four-foot horn in the middle of its forehead, so sharp and strong that it tosses in the air or impales whatever it attacks. It often fights with the elephant and throws it to the ground after wounding it in the belly. It has such strength that it can be captured by no hunter's ability, but, as those who have written about the natures of animals claim, if a virgin girl is set before a unicorn, as the beast approaches, she may open her lap and it will lay its head there with all ferocity put aside, and thus lulled and disarmed it may be captured.

Physiologus

(translated by Michael J. Curley, published by the University of Chicago Press, 1979)

In Deuteronomy Moses said while blessing Joseph, 'His beauty is that of the firstling bull, and his horns are the horns of the unicorn'. The monoceras, that is, the unicorn, has this nature: he is a small animal like the kid, is exceedingly shrewd, and has one horn in the middle of his head. The hunter cannot approach him because he is extremely strong. How then do they hunt the beast? Hunters place a chaste virgin before him. He bounds forth into her lap and she warms and nourishes the animal and takes him into the palace of the kings.

The unicorn has one horn because the Savior said, 'I and the Father are one'. 'For he has raised up a horn of salvation for us in the house of his servant David'. Coming down from heaven, he came into the womb of the Virgin Mary.

Albertus Magnus (1193-1280)
On Animals

Monoceros

The monoceros is composed of many animals, makes a horrible lowing, has a horse's body, an elephant's feet, a pig's tail, and it has a hart's head in the middle of which is a bright splendid horn of great beauty, four feet long and so sharp that it easily punctures everything it strikes. Never, or rarely, can it be tamed and come under the power of men while it lives, for when it views itself conquered it furiously kills itself.

Unicorn

The unicorn is an animal of moderate size for its strength, of boxwood colour and with cloven hooves, that lives in mountains and deserts with a very long horn which it sharpens on rocks and can even pierce an elephant and is not afraid of hunters. This great animal Pompey sent to Rome.

On the other hand, they say that this animal venerates virgin girls so much that when it sees them it becomes docile and when it is asleep nearby can be captured and bound. It also may be captured when it is a young chick and then domesticated.

Marco Polo (1254-1329)
The Travels of Marco Polo, The Venetian

(Translated by William Marsden, published by Cox and Baylis, 1818)

In the country are many wild elephants and rhinoceroses, which latter are much inferior in size to the elephant, but their feet are similar. Their hide resembles that of the buffalo. In the middle of the forehead they have a single horn; but with this weapon they do not injure those whom they attack, employing only for this purpose their tongue, which is armed with long, sharp spines, and their knees or feet; their mode of assault being to trample upon the person, and then to lacerate him with the tongue. Their head is like that of a wild boar, and they carry it low towards the ground. They take delight in muddy pools, and are filthy in their habits. They are not of that description of animals which suffer themselves to be taken by maidens, as our people suppose, but are quite of a contrary nature.

Sir John Mandeville (14TH Century)
The Travels of Sir John Mandeville

(Translated by C.W.R.D. Moseley, published by Penguin, 1983)

There are also other kinds of animals, as big as horses; they are called *louherans*, and some call them *touez*, and others *odenthos*. They have black heads and three horns on the brow, as sharp as swords; their bodies are yellow. They are marvellously cruel beasts, and will chase and kill the elephant.

Ganda in Gujarat

By the beginning of the sixteenth century a trade route had been established between India and Portugal for shipping spices to Europe. Vasco de Gama had shown the way but it was Afonso de Albuquerque who conquered the Indian coast, developing the Portuguese Empire and raising Portuguese forts to assert and protect their rule. Fleets of ships filled with spices – black pepper, cloves, cinnamon – crossed the Indian Ocean on the Winter Monsoon winds, arriving four months later into Lisbon and delivering goods to India House, alongside King Manuel I's palace.

As well as spices, the ships would bring back other goods – exotic ornaments and animals – as gifts for the king. And as well as monopolising the spice trade, Albuquerque's intention was to squash Islam and impose Christianity.

...

In his book *The Unicorn*, which is about the rhinoceros or kara-dann in Islamic iconography, Richard Ettinghausen notes a recurrent quirk in Islamic medieval bestiaries, which he says probably originated from Al-Jahiz's ninth century *Book of Animals*. The rhinoceros, it says, has a long gestation period of seven years, towards the end of which the unborn calf sometimes pops his head out to graze then pops back in again.

...

Pope Leo X was only elected the previous year, 1513. He was of the Medici family, son of Lorenzo the Magnificent, and he was a very different sort of pontiff from his predecessor. This Medici Pope was implausibly well-connected and wealthy, a lover of the arts, of poetry, improvisation, music, goldwork and painting, and he continued to support or commission works from some of the most celebrated figures in history – Michelangelo (nanchakus[5]), Leonardo (katanas[6]), and especially Raphael (sai).[7] He slept well and ate well and spent the Vatican's money extremely well.

5   Using the spelling from the original 1984 Eastman and Laird comics, which did their bit for mythologizing ninjas.

6   The original comic of 1984 describes Leonardo's weapon as a katana, the famous sword of the samurai, but officious martial artists point out they are more like ninjatos, a twentieth century imagining.

7   The Medici Pope commissioned most of the turtles, although his favourite by far was Raphael, whose work, as a result, can be found throughout the Vatican, including a portrait of the pontiff himself. At the same time, an ageing Leonardo was living at the Villa Belvedere. Between Leonardo's home and the Palace an elaborate series of courtyards was being developed, and it was near here that Leo X would keep his elephant.

The turtles didn't really like one another very much. Leonardo and Michelangelo avoided contact, to such an extent (according to Vasari) that one would leave town if the other was due to arrive. Similarly, there are anecdotes of Michelangelo and Raphael exchanging insults, Michelangelo mocking the fawning students following Raphael about and Raphael mocking the lack of anyone following Michelangelo about.

Pope Leo X does not seem to have cared very much for either Leonardo or Michelangelo, even though he had known Michelangelo since childhood and the artist had enjoyed the favour of both Leo X's father, Lorenzo the Magnificent, and his predecessor, Pope Julius II, who commissioned the ceiling of the Sistine Chapel.

Only one of the turtles appears to have painted a rhinoceros; Raphael ('cool but crude') in his *The Creation of the Animals*, painted just a couple of years after the death of the Ganda. The rhino is poking his head out from behind a palm tree where it appears to be trying to hide – along with an elephant and a unicorn – from God, who probably would have spotted them if He wasn't busy trying not to step on a tiger.

In the 1987 cartoon, one of the turtles was also a rhinoceros. Leonardo was voiced by Cam Clarke, the same actor as the mutant baddie Rocksteady. Rocksteady is usually portrayed as one of the African rhino species, with two horns.

Donatello, fine artist though he might be, is an anachronism in the television series. He was of an earlier generation to the other turtles, and died before two of them were even born.

Afonso de Albuquerque had wanted to build a fort on Diu Island, off the coast of Gujarat, for some time, but negotiations with the Sultan, Muzafar II, had not been going well. So in 1514 he sent a couple of his ambassadors, Diogo Fernandez de Béja and James Teixeira, to meet with this Muslim king and negotiate the deal.

They took all sorts of gifts for the Sultan, including a gold-sheathed dagger, expensive cloths, Chinese ornaments, a gilded ewer and some twenty horses.

The troupe arrived in March and were well-entertained in the Gujarati port of Surat, exchanging gifts and messages with the city's ruler and awkwardly negotiating the expectations of hospitality. At length, the Portuguese were granted leave to travel across Gujarat to Champaner, arriving in early April. At Champaner they were entertained by another dignitary, feasting for days before they were able to head off again in search of the king. They would have to travel another hundred miles to Ahmedabad, accompanied by a range of horsemen and distinguished people.

This was not to be a swift negotiation.

...

In Islamic art there is a long tradition of unicorns or rhinoceroses of various shapes and sizes. Writing in the eleventh century, the insatiable scholar Al-Biruni produced a critical study of the religion, geography, science and astronomy of India, in which he describes the rhinoceros, or *ganda*, with more accuracy than Western contemporaries:

> The *ganda* exists in large numbers in India, more particularly about the Ganges. It is of the build of a buffalo, has a black scaly skin, and dewlaps hanging down under the chin. It has three yellow hoofs on each foot, the biggest one forward, the others on both sides. The tail is not long; the eyes lie low, farther down the cheek than is the case with all other animals. On the top of the nose there is a single horn which is bent upwards. The Brahmins have the privilege of eating the flesh of the *ganda*. I have myself witnessed how an elephant coming across a young *ganda* was attacked by it. The *ganda* wounded with its horn a forefoot of the elephant, and threw it down on its face.

...

One of the Pope's greatest pleasures was hunting. In spite of canonical restrictions and the disapproval of his peers, the new Pope could not resist the hunt in any of its forms. He would ride out with a company of more than a hundred in pursuit of wild boar, hares, wolves, porcupines, goats and deer. He had land set aside for breeding rabbits for his ferrets. He kept a range of birds of prey, including peregrines, merlins and goshawks, and an aviary of doves and herons for the raptors to kill. He would hunt pheasants and partridges, fish for eels at Bolsena, even catch songbirds and finches.

...

At Ahmedabad, Albuquerque's ambassadors were told to wait further while Muzafar was out hunting. Then, at last, they were summoned to the court, accompanied by a great troupe of horsemen and buglers. The king was reclining on a sofa. They exchanged gifts, talked about the weather and then were requested to leave.

The following day, pleasantries dispatched, the Portuguese were called back to the court to talk business. But rather than Muzafar discussing the proposed fort of Diu Island with the ambassadors, the king disappeared, sending his trusted minister Khudawand Khan to give the bad news.

...

'Since God has given us the papacy, my Giuliano,' Pope Leo X told his cousin on succeeding to the papacy, 'let us enjoy it.'

...

In Sindbad the Sailor's second voyage the hero falls asleep on an island and his ship leaves without him. He discovers a giant bird, the Rukh, so large that its egg is like a great dome and it feeds on elephants. Sindbad tries to use the bird to escape, tying himself to its foot with his turban. Following a quick succession of adventures with the giant bird, vultures, venomous serpents and diamonds, Sindbad finds himself in the company of merchants and in another strange land:

Upon the plains roamed the wild rhinoceros, of which wonderful tales are told by people who return from unknown lands. This beast impales an elephant upon its horn with ease, and wanders thus, with little hindrance to its pasturing, until the fat of the elephant, melting in the heat of the sun, and flowing down into its eyes, renders it blind; whereupon it seeks the seashore and lies down until such time as the rukh may find it and carry both it and the elephant away as a morsel for its young.

...

The new Pope received gifts and ostentatious displays of obeisance from rulers all across Europe, and Manuel knew he would be competing for the Medici's attention. But Manuel had a significant advantage: his trade routes. The Portuguese practically monopolised trade with India, employing a great military force to maintain their position. And it was not only India. They were trading with coastal Africa and beginning to approach China and Japan. Manuel had access to a continent of wonders the likes of which even the famous Medici would never have seen before, including wild animals.

In March 1514, at the same time as Diogo Fernandez de Béja and James Teixeira were landing in Surat on the other side of the world, another Portuguese ambassador, the celebrated explorer Tristao da Cunha, was making a dramatic impression on Rome on behalf of the Portuguese king. Along with a large company of distinguished Portuguese naval men, poets and scientists, Tristao da Cunha took a choice selection of creatures from Manuel's own menagerie to augment the papal zoo, including big cats, parrots, horses and Hanno, a white Indian elephant.[8]

---

8   Silvio Bedini brilliantly researched this elephant and wrote a book about it, *The Pope's Elephant*.

The gifts were a generous, entertaining gesture as well as a demonstration of the growing reach of the Portuguese empire.

...

There would be no fortress. Muzafar had been informed that the fort was a way for Albuquerque to challenge the Sultan's rule and gain further strategic advantage and control of the region. On no account would he give his permission.[9]

Sending Khudawand Khan was a wise diplomatic move. After a few days cooling off period, Muzafar called the visitors back to court. Since he had only had pleasant exchanges with Albuquerque's men so far it was easy for him to continue in the same vein, greeting them as friends. The disagreement had been with Khudawand, not with the Sultan.

So when they arrived at court the Portuguese were presented with silk clothes, daggers and belts, a letter for Albuquerque from the Sultan, and the promise of a special gift, currently being held for them at Champaner. A *ganda*. The Sultan said he would forward the *ganda* to the coastal city of Surat, from where they were due to be sailing back to Goa.

The weather had other plans. By the time they reached Surat it was May and the Gujarat monsoon rains were coming in. Diogo Fernandez de Béja, James Teixeira and Ganda were stranded in Surat until September. Albuquerque

---

9   History proved Muzafar right. In the 1530s, one of Muzafar's sons was Sultan of Gujarat. He succeeded a string of brothers who had met sticky ends. Under his rule an alliance was struck with the Portuguese that led to their 400-year rule of the region.

greeted them in anger. He had given strict instructions for them to be back in Goa before the rains. Now they wouldn't be able to leave for Portugal until the new year and the Winter Monsoon winds. They had to spend another four months here – and now they had a rhinoceros to deal with.

...

In January 1515, Ganda was loaded onboard the *Nossa Senhora da Ajuda*, Our Lady of Help, bound for Europe.

Carreira Da India, 1515
(January-May 20th)

I.

    Ganda, in the belly
    of Our Lady

the smell of cinnamon, cloves
and sandalwood

        Hail, Star of the Sea
        a single drop of blood

        from the night sky

cord blood
rice and straw

her iron cord tightening
around his legs

    blown like a nicker nut
    on the winter monsoons

        Solve vincla reis,
        profer lumen

II.

It has been four months. One hundred and twenty days. A drop of light penetrates Our Lady's creaking darkness on the banks of the Tagus before the Palace of Ribeira. 'You are premature,' says the king on the shore. Smells of fish, waste and old fruit. People congeal into crowds.

The rhinoceros – sea-worn and unsteady – is led to the trade stores of the palace's India House. 'You have been delivered too soon. You will have to wait for your cage.'

Hail, star of the sea, nurturing mother and eternal virgin, blessed gate of heaven.

Babar Versus Rataxes

The time has come to play our hand;
the army's ready now here's the plan:
at dawn we march for the Elephant Land.

By night we'll reach the city wall;
by morning we shall rule them all.

Rataxes

If we remember anything about the TV series *Babar* it might be the antagonism between King Babar the elephant and Lord Rataxes the rhinoceros; two large, powerful animals representing opposing points of view. Babar is the ~~benelephant~~ benevolent enlightened ruler of the gentle elephant folk of Celesteville and Elephant Land, while Rataxes is the cruel, unreasonable, belligerent brute of Rhinoland.

This antagonism was scarcely present in Jean de Brunhoff's original picture books, of which he wrote just a handful. In the very first, *The Story of Babar the Little Elephant*, the only rhinoceros is an unnamed guest at the wedding of Babar and Celeste, dancing with a hippo in the crowd and smiling. In the second title, *Babar's Travels*, we see the origins of their enmity, but this was not instigated by Rataxes the rhinoceros. Rather, it was the fault of the elephants.

Arthur, the child cousin of Babar, finds Rataxes sleeping and ties a firework to his tail. It goes off with a great bang, amusing the young elephant and terrifying, then enraging, the rhinoceros, who responds by destroying the Great Forest and declaring war on the elephants while Babar is away on holiday.

When Babar returns he finds his land conquered and his people badly beaten. To restore his kingdom and scare away the rhinos, Babar makes the other elephants put wigs and make-up on their huge arses. In this way the elephants capture Rataxes, the war ends, and the rhinos do not appear again in Jean de Brunhoff's books.

The serious antagonism between the rhinoceroses and elephants in subsequent iterations of the Babar stories was introduced by Brunhoff's son, Laurent, who took over the characters and wrote dozens and dozens more Babar books, including *Babar's Battle*, which was, of course, a battle with Rataxes. Laurent developed the idea of inter-special belligerence, making Rataxes a proud, avaricious dictator who wants to conquer Celesteville, a position some distance from the picture drawn by his father Jean.

This exaggerated hatred of Rataxes for Babar and the desire to conquer and own Celesteville was further amplified by the TV series, which ran over some six seasons. Here, from the very beginning, Rataxes and Babar are in competition, racing to build a city, then to fly to the moon, with Rataxes constantly trying to capture or overthrow Babar. Rataxes is a simple narrative foil to Babar's endeavours.

The popular 1989 *Babar: the Movie* cemented this antagonism, adding an evil laugh and a vaguely piratic West-country accent to Rataxes's despotic qualities. The movie begins with the rhinos (dressed in something like conquistadour armour) invading an elephant village, capturing slaves to build Rataxes's city while screaming wildly and setting fire to homes. Hidden in the jungle, Babar is wearing his white hunter outfit.

Zidan Aulia Chandramata 1 year ago
YEA RHINO TEACH THEN WHO'S BOSS

👍 3   👎   REPLY

View reply ∨

The antagonism between rhinos and elephants is fantastical, yet Babar versus Rataxes is just one of the more recent versions of the story. Elephants and rhinoceroses have been facing off in literature for millennia.

Pliny describes the rhinoceros as a great 'Enemy to the Elephant. He fileth this Horn against hard Stones, and so prepareth himself to fight; and in his Conflict he aimeth principally at the Belly, which he knoweth to be the tenderest Part.'

The story is repeated down the centuries. The sixth century traveller Cosmas Indicopleustes, for example, writes that the rhinoceros is 'altogether a most terrible animal, and is especially hostile to the elephant', while Isidore of Seville in his *Etymologies* a few decades later writes how, 'With the elephant it often wrangles, wounding its gut and throwing it down.' Sir John Mandeville, fourteenth century travel writer (commonly thought not to have travelled to any of the places of which he writes), described rhinoceroses as 'marvellously cruel beasts, and will chase and kill the elephant.'

SquidKidDavid Eng 2 years ago

Elephant: waassup man?!? trynna wrastle??
Rhino: BISH!! Back the hell up!
Elephant: Jeezus, I was just playin.. chill.

👍 5 👎   REPLY

This legendary rivalry was of such fascination to Europe that now and then pachyderms were brought together to test the claim, albeit never to great effect.

On the 3rd June (my birthday – I was minus 465 that year), just two weeks after Ganda had arrived in Portugal, King Manuel constructed an arena in the courtyard between the Ribeira Palace and India House for the battle. It was made a festival day and was anticipated all across Lisbon.

Ganda's handler Oçem led the rhino out and waited in the arena for the elephant, one of a handful of elephants given to the Portuguese King. A crowd surrounded them, including the royal family.

The elephant was released. It entered the arena, raised its trunk, eyed up the rhino, turned tail and fled. So ended Lisbon's battle of the monsters, 1515.

bahrul bahar 2 years ago

Feels like watching dinosaurs fight

👍 305 👎   REPLY

View 22 replies ⌄

The search for the superlative, for the greatest, the fiercest, persists. 'Elephant versus Rhino.' 'Lion versus Tiger.' 'Samurai versus Ninja.' 'Alien versus Predator.' 'King Kong versus Godzilla.' 'Hulk versus Thor.' 'Ali versus Tyson.' Whole TV series, YouTube channels and cartoon movies have been dedicated to these speculations. We want to be able to say 'there is no greater than…'

An aspect of this is the awe the spectator and ancient reader might feel when confronted by a rhinoceros or an elephant for the first time. When introduced to a monster, a hero, a superlative being, there is a feeling of wonder at its extent – its power and size. (This 'awe' or 'wonder' is a field currently being researched, in part, through 'elevation theory'.)

But why do we want them to fight? Why is that word 'versus' so frequently used? It is as though having multiple superlative beings compromises the original sense of awe, and so the pleasure we might derive from it. The heroic uncertainty is unsettling. We want a resolution of the pattern.

'There can be only one,' runs the tagline of *Highlander*, the tension of its franchise all the while relying on there being multiple individuals vying to be that 'one'.

The final episode of the *Babar* TV series sees a cooling of the elephant-rhino fervour. The episode, entitled 'Mango Madness', is about the virtue of political dishonesty – telling lies in order to get a good trade deal. In the end the young elephant Flora cries from confusion, Rataxes makes her a balloon elephant and they all dress as fruits.

ani lata 11 months ago

Very beautiful videos

👍 👎   REPLY

View reply ⌄

Aj Basit 1 month ago

Very good

👍 3 👎   REPLY

swapan Ruhidas 1 month ago

Bad

👍 4 👎   REPLY

Jdor D 1 year ago

Great video as usual. .."Yeshua / Jesus is the way "

👍 2 👎   REPLY

Sadanand Rajbhar 1 month ago

k

Penni Dreadful

Giovanni Giacomo Penni was a Florentine doctor who appears to have written a few accounts of current affairs from the court of the Medici Pope in the early parts of the sixteenth century, including a twenty-one-stanza poetry pamphlet, 'Forma & Natura & Costumi de lo Rinocerothe stato condutto importogallo dal Capitanio de larmata del Re & altre belle cose condutte dalle insule nouamente trouate', about Ganda in 1515.

The poem is extraordinary for a couple of reasons. To begin with, it is accompanied by one of the earliest surviving depictions of the rhinoceros – a comic sort of woodcut that seems to be wearing a spotty blanket. But it is also interesting for the swiftness of production. Ganda arrived in Portugal in May and the poem was printed in July. That gives very little time for news to travel from Lisbon to Rome, then to the Leonine court, then to be turned into such an elephant of a poem as this and to be printed and distributed.

The poem itself is mostly courtly drivel with a few perfunctory apologies from its author for being such a poor poet, but in the middle are the following stanzas, translated here by Sophy Downes. They do not mention the damp squib of a scuffle in the King's courtyard, which might suggest the news hadn't reached Rome by the time of composition, although, having said this, would Penni have bothered to include such a bland moment in his poetic confectionary?

THE APPEARANCE, CHARACTER, AND HABITS OF THE RHINOCEROS WHICH WAS BROUGHT TO PORTUGAL BY THE CAPTAIN OF THE KING'S FLEET AND OTHER FINE THINGS BROUGHT BACK FROM THE NEWLY DISCOVERED ISLANDS (verses 3-10)

I hear a captain has just returned
from sultry Calcutta to Lisbon town,
his three ships packed to the decks with wealth
from which he intends to win great renown.
He praises the Lord for his prosperous voyage
to whom every Christian soul bows down.
His name is Alfonso of Albuquerque,
by King Emmanuel deemed exceedingly worthy.

In 1500 at the end of May
Alfonso arrived, so say those who scribble
that kind of thing, or rather fifteen years
later, in fact—but that's a quibble.
And all should thank this courageous man
for the wisdom with which he loaded his ship, I'll
just mention the gold, the jewels, the spices,
and the marvellous monsters of many devices.

In council our captain presented the king
with a very vast and redoubtable creature,
merely the sight of which could strike
fear to the core of the bravest nature.
The beast has flesh as tough as an anvil,
feet with three toes, and its other features
are skin the colour of rigor mortis
and legs as rough as a scaly tortoise.

Rhinoceros! is this creature called —
in every way a formidable animal.
On the end of his nose sits a tidy horn
with which he does damage so fierce and tyrannical
that his captors fix a chain round his leg
to drag him about. His body's a shambles
of mulish ears and bovine knees,
but they say he performs incredible deeds.

By its nature the rhinoceros feels
for elephants a stubborn hatred,
and often gores them with his horn —
likewise all beasts of size inflated.
But smaller creatures he ignores
with judgment most discriminating.
The elephant too is highly intelligent,
which is why their encounters are often inelegant.

Already at Rome in Pompey's games
the bold rhinoceros is mentioned,
and later in the Colosseum
they say his feats drew much attention —
transfixing each rival til the crowd
prayed to the gods for intervention
to deplete his strength. And his thunderous breath,
the Romans write, frightened dogs to death.

Pliny and Martial both make mention
of this noble and attractive beast;
he is also found in the Morgante,
although its author just repeats

that he hates the elephant intensely.
If the rhino comes to Rome our peace
might be disturbed, but we'll find a way
to let everyone enjoy his stay.

Alfonso brought thousands of other beasts,
bizarre and strange, including wagons
of Barbary apes and wild baboons
which he gave as gifts to the Portuguese barons.
But as I have many more things to say,
I'll keep this brief—I do not plan on
dragging out my speech and boring you
when I'm sure you have other things to do.

The Monk and the Rhinoceros

In Eugene Ionesco's play *Rhinoceros* the inhabitants of a provincial town turn into rhinoceroses. The only person not to succumb to this 'rhinoceritis' is Bergenger, a lazy, self-questioning, heavy-drinking and sympathisable everyman who features in several of Ionesco's plays. Here he is in ideological opposition to the dumb, conforming rhinoceroses rampaging through the town. As well as being associated with the Theatre of the Absurd, *Rhinoceros* is a critique of the dehumanising effects of the kind of fascist totalitarianism in which Ionesco grew up.

The poet and Trappist monk Thomas Merton writes about Ionesco's rhinoceroses in his essay 'Rain and the Rhinoceros', relating Bergenger's nonconformity to the eremitic life. So on the one hand there is the violent conformity of the rhinoceroses, and on the other the benign solitude of Bergenger. Merton translates a wonderful passage from a talk Ionesco gave in front of a group of French and German writers:[10]

> The universal and modern man is the man in a rush (i.e. a rhinoceros), a man who has no time, who is a prisoner of necessity, who cannot understand that a thing might perhaps be without usefulness; nor does he understand that, at bottom, it is the useful that may be a useless and back-breaking burden. If one does not understand the

---

10   A translation of the talk by Donald Watson can be found in *Notes and Counter Notes*, London: Caldar and Boyars, 1964, pgs 151-158.

usefulness of the useless and the uselessness of the useful, one cannot understand art.

Ionesco goes on to say: 'Forms of rhinoceritis of every kind, from left and right, are there to threaten humanity when men have no time to think or collect themselves.'

Merton focuses on the violence of the herd. We assume, he says, that it is the outsider who hates those who conform – the herd – those excluding the outsider – but perhaps the opposite is the case. Within conformity, he says, the dialectic of power and need, of submission and satisfaction, ends by being a dialectic of hate. Collectivity needs not only to absorb everyone it can, but also implicitly to hate and destroy whoever cannot be absorbed. Paradoxically, one of the needs of collectivity is to reject certain classes, or races, or groups, in order to strengthen its own self-awareness by hating them instead of absorbing them.

Independence from the herd is a condition for the true love of all people.

'Rain and the Rhinoceros' is a beautiful piece, and both Merton's and Ionesco's works are interesting for their inversion of one common attribute of the rhinoceros's story. That is, here the rhinoceros is a herd animal, a symbol of the dumb violence of the collective, when usually it is the opposite, a solitary creature. Merton would have been aware of the *Rhinoceros Horn Sutra*, an ancient Buddhist text about the monastic life with the refrain 'one should wander solitary as a rhinoceros horn'.[11]

11   I'm following KR Norman's translation (found in the Pali Text Society edition and in the Penguin Classics title *Buddhist Scriptures*) of 'rhinoceros horn'. Other translations say that it is not the 'horn' that is solitary but the rhinoceros itself. That is, they say the phrase should be 'solitary as a rhinoceros'. The debate hinges on a discrepancy between the ancient text

The first passage of the sutra is on violence:

Laying aside violence in respect of all beings, not harming even one of them, one should not wish for a son, let alone a companion. One should wander solitary as a rhinoceros horn.

---

and the ancient commentary on the ancient text. The text itself uses a word (khaggavisāṇa) that could refer to either the rhinoceros or its horn, while the commentary asserts that it is definitely the horn that is solitary. The issue seems to be, how lonely can a horn be when it has its rhinoceros attached?

Rhinoceros Unicornis:
a deviation on the unicorn

The pushmi-pullyu 'had no tail, but a head at each end, and sharp horns on each head.' He was one of the rarest animals in the world and has since become extinct. In *The Story of Dr Doolittle*, the pushmi-pullyu explains its heritage, being related 'to the Abyssinian Gazelles and the Asiatic Chamois – on my mother's side. My father's great–grandfather was the last of the Unicorns.'[12]

…

Psalm 92 is said to have been spoken by Adam. 'For, lo, thine enemies, O Lord, for, lo, thine enemies shall perish; all the workers of iniquity shall be scattered. But my horn shalt thou exalt like *the horn of* an unicorn.'

…

'I always thought they were fabulous monsters', says the Unicorn in Lewis Carroll's *Through the Looking Glass*, having seen a child – Alice – for the first time. 'Well … if you'll believe in me, I'll believe in you. Is that a bargain?' The Unicorn is taking a break from fighting the Lion, the characters enacting the nursery rhyme in which the two – one representing Scotland (the unicorn) the other England (the lion) – fight and then eat cake. The rhyme is said to derive from when King James VI of Scotland also became King James

---

12   In the 1967 movie with Rex Harrison the Pushmi-pullyu has a llama at each end.

I of England, in 1603, and the royal coats of arms were fused together, taking one unicorn from the Scottish and one Lion from the English. It remains the coat of arms for the United Kingdom.

...

Thomas Browne's essay from the mid-seventeenth century, 'of the Unicorn's horn', troubles the claims of Browne's contemporaries (as well as the claims of medieval and ancient writers) that the unicorn's horn has magical properties. Aelian had said that drinking from the horn was an antidote to poison. Browne says that Aelian is the only ancient writer to make this statement.[13]

...

St Basil said Christ was a unicorn.

...

In the second century a new collection of allegorical Christian natural histories began to circulate, known as the *Physiologus*. They appeared first in Greek, then in Ethiopian, Syrian, Armenian and Latin. The *Physiologus* was the early Middle Age equivalent of an international bestseller, and its contents directly informed centuries of subsequent bestiaries,

---

13   Had ancient Chinese texts like the *Shen Nong Ben Cao Ling* been available to Browne he would have found an interesting parallel between the unicorn and the rhinoceros. Ground rhinoceros horn was said to have a similar application in the treatment against toxins there, with further uses in innumerable ailments.

including the wonderful animal pages put together by Isidore of Seville (560-636AD) in his *Etymologies*. The *Physiologus* contains information about animals, followed by Christian interpretations about what this information means – what the behaviour of the animals, or the stories of the animals, might signify. For example, of the hedgehog, the author begins by telling the reader that:

> [the hedgehog] climbs up to the grape on the vine and then throws down the berries (that is, the grapes) onto the ground. Then he rolls himself over on them, fastening the fruit of the vine to his quills, and carries it off to his young and discards the plucked stalk.

(Surely the best detail here is that he discards the stalk.)

The moral is that 'you, O Christian' should 'stand watch over your spiritual vineyard from which you stock your spiritual cellar.'

...

One of Thomas Browne's problems is the range of obviously different horns claiming to be that of the unicorn. Similarly, in the history of the Indian rhinoceros, monoceros and unicorn, we find descriptions that vary considerably, the result of the fact that none of the authors of these descriptions ever saw an Indian rhinoceros, monoceros or unicorn.

...

A lesson we might derive from the *Physiologus* is that by close observation of the natural world we can better comprehend the divine.

...

Raphael painted a portrait of a young woman with a very little unicorn sitting docilely on her lap. This is one of the *Physiologus*'s tiny unicorns, the size of a baby goat and a symbol of the young woman's chastity. Ten years later, Albrecht Dürer made an iron etching of a man abducting a naked woman while riding a unicorn. The unicorn, like all of Dürer's horses, is a burly, turbulent creature, its horn curving the opposite way to the previous year's rhinoceros.

...

In Photios's abridgement of Ctesias, the single-horned 'wild ass' is said to be the size of a horse. When Aelian comes to rewrite Ctesias he mentions this 'wild ass' the size of a horse, but also another, an actual horse with a single horn.

...

The *Physiologus* assumes that the unicorn and the monoceros are the same thing. Isidore of Seville says that the rhinoceros, monoceros and the unicorn are all the same. Marco Polo assumes that the rhinoceros and the unicorn are the same thing.

...

The association of the unicorn with goodness and innocence – whether that of the young virgin or that of Christ – has moved the iconography further and further from that of the rhinoceros. In the twentieth century, Disney's *Fantasia* presented us with cutesy confectionary-coloured juvenile unicorns, the prototypes of *My Little Pony's* cutesy confectionary-coloured Glory, Moondancer, Sunbeam and Twilight from their 1983 Unicorn series. That same year *My Little Pony* appears to have started the association of rainbows with unicorns, launching their Rainbow Unicorn figure series with Windy and Moonstone.

In 2017 Starbucks created a limited edition 'Unicorn Frappuccino' – white, pink and blue – pastel colours, rainbow swirls.

...

When Voldemort drank the unicorn's blood, it was the blood of Christ and it tasted of mango syrup.

...

The medieval bestiaries based their descriptions on the ancient works, especially the fragments of the *Physiologus* and its sources, repeating the errors and adding further allegorical layers and illuminations. Still none of them had seen the beast.

When India was opened up to Europe by the Portuguese trade routes the fantastical tales of the Far East were exposed. Some people allowed that Ganda was the real rhinoceros, monoceros and unicorn, but others continued to point to the differences between the modern Indian rhinoceros and ancient descriptions of single-horned beasts and said there *must* be more.

...

Christ is a rhinoceros.

Interlude On Oçem

There is nothing much to say about Oçem.

We know that Oçem was given a suit of clothes by order of Alphonse d'Albuquerque for the long journey from Goa to Portugal. And we know that Oçem's fate was shackled to Ganda's, as Ganda was shackled to the sinking ship. Beyond that, there is nothing much to say about Oçem.

What does Oçem mean? Is it a Portuguese spelling of a name we might anglicise as Osam or Osham? There is an Osam Hill in Gujarat. Does that help?

Then, why was Oçem chosen to leave India for Europe? Was Oçem keen to visit Portugal? Was he escaping India? Or did he hope to return home one day? Was he ambitious? Was he shipped against his will? Did he love Ganda? Had he raised Ganda? Did he have family? Was he a child or an adult? Did he like his Portuguese sailor suit?

And is that Oçem in the background of Francesco Granacci's 'Joseph Presents his Father and his Brothers to the Pharaoh', following the rhinoceros? A shadow with bowed head but fists raised? Or is he reading? Or is he holding a chain?

There is nothing much to say about Oçem.

Dürer's Rhinoceros

I

(Image after Dürer's woodcut) [CF Sherratt]

A print of Albrecht Dürer's rhinoceros woodcut is held in the British Museum. It is roughly 8 inches high and 12 inches wide and has letterpress printed text above it. The rhinoceros is armour-plated and spotted like a giraffe, with a pronounced saddle and patterned rib cage. As well as the single horn on the rhinoceros's nose, there is a second, decorative mini-horn in between the shoulder blades, while its face is a landscape of bony lumps.

One of the most wonderful things about Dürer's rhinoceros is that he never saw a rhinoceros. The sketch and resulting woodcut were created from a description and, presumably, some kind of image that would have been sent to Nuremberg from Lisbon along with a report on the arrival of the sensational monster as soon as it arrived.

Dürer was not the only artist to create an image from these reports. Two others stand out: Hans Burgmair's hairy rhino and the baggy-skinned sketch that accompanied Penni's poem. The differences between the three suggest that they might have been based on slightly different images, although the similarities are just as fascinating.

The most obvious difference between Dürer's rhinoceros and the other two is that Dürer's is not bound around its front legs. Both the Burgmair and the Penni images are tethered. Dürer and Burgmair share the most, including an identical stance, a bristly chin and a bare, stony setting. Dürer and Penni share the gnarly face markings. All three images emphasise the rhino's three toes and have a hairy tail, with giraffe spots, and they all show the skin almost separated into plates – most notably in the Dürer image. But then the artists add their own details. Penni's rhino looks like it is wearing a badly fitting rug and a helmet. Burgmair's is softer, with a mane like a horse. Dürer added scales to the legs, like chainmail, and it's not at all clear where he got the idea for the extra horn between the shoulder blades. Does this show mistrust of the original image and description? Or was Dürer adding the horn based on the more familiar African rhinoceros's two horns?

(after Burgmair's hairy rhinoceros) [CF Sherratt]

In truth, Dürer's success with animals was mixed. His 'Wing of a Roller' is stunningly, madly beautiful, as are the wings of the cherubs in 'Madonna with the Siskin' and the fur of his 'Hare'. On the other hand, he struggled with lions. Both of Dürer's most famous lions – in 'Saint Jerome in his Cell' and in 'Penitent Saint Jerome' – have oddly distended foreheads and strange smirks. The horses of 'The Four Horsemen of the Apocalypse' look a bit like their faces have all been chewed (but then so do the human figures), while his dogs are a real mixed bag.

Two of the most overlooked Dürer beasts appear in the background of his 'Adoration of the Magi': the ox and the ass. These two are staples in the iconography of the nativity scene, and here we see the gingery-brown ox calmly looking at Jesus (who has a weirdly bulbous head and tiny pinched face) while the ass is baring its teeth with its ears back, braying. The pairing of these two has a long history that has been written about by saints and popes alike, including St Augustine, St Jerome and Pope Benedict XVI. And when St Francis was staging his own Christmas story in the hermitage caves of Greccio he brought in a real ox and an ass for authenticity. (Francis's is said to have been the first ever Christmas nativity, beginning the tradition.)

Not all accounts are in agreement, but the consensus seems to be that the ox is the clean animal (in the Biblical sense) and is associated with the Jewish people, while the ass is the unclean and represents the Gentiles who would not hear Christ's teachings. The ass in Dürer's painting is not just deaf, but clearly hostile to Christ.

Anyway, Dürer's ox has lovely hair. Dürer always painted excellent hair – beards especially. The colours and lusciousness of the beards of 'The Apostle James the Elder' and his 1521 'Saint Jerome' are almost too tactilely inviting to resist.

(after the woodcut on Penni's poem) [CF Sherratt]

The Gothic script text of Dürer's rhinoceros gets the date wrong, stating that Ganda landed on 1st May 1513. Presumably this was an error of the letterpress printer, inserting a 3 instead of another 5.

The British Museum offers a full translation of the German printed above the woodcut:

> On 1 May 1513 was brought from India to the great and powerful king Emanuel of Portugal at Lisbon a live animal called a rhinoceros. His form is here represented. It has the colour of a speckled tortoise and it is covered with thick scales. It is like an elephant in size, but lower on its legs and almost invulnerable. It has a strong sharp horn on its nose which it sharpens on stones. The stupid animal is the elephant's deadly enemy. The elephant is very frightened of it as, when they meet, it runs with its head down between its front legs and gores the stomach of the elephant and throttles it, and the elephant cannot fend it off. Because the animal is so well armed, there is nothing that the elephant can do to it. It is also said that the rhinoceros is fast, lively and cunning.

The description of the skin being like that of a tortoise or turtle (*Schildkrot*) in colour explains the giraffe spots, while in real life the rhinoceros has bumps, or tubercles, over its legs and flanks. The Babar-Rataxes antagonism remains a key feature, in spite of the let-down in Lisbon, and it is tempting to imagine that the emphasis on how frightened elephants are of rhinoceroses is a reference to that moment in the square outside Manuel's menagerie.

The word 'stupid' probably isn't the best translation of the old German 'sieg', which others have translated as *victorious* or *triumphant*.

(after Dürer's pen and ink rhinoceros) [CF Sherratt]

Without Dürer's sensational woodcut rhinoceros the story of Ganda might never have been told. Yet in some ways this rhinoceros is not Ganda at all. Dürer's rhinoceros is liberated, untethered, and is intended to be representative of a species, an example of the rhinoceros-as-such. Yes, an example of the rhinoceros-as-such created from an artistic kind of Chinese whispers and an ancient mosaic of zoological writing, on top of which Dürer layered his own fantasticism. A lust for the spectacle, for the impossible, the magical, the superlative. Ganda only dimly haunts these depictions of Ganda.

King Manuel Considering Taking a Rhinoceros on a Ship to see the Pope (after Francis Bacon)

For

The Pope will like your rhinoceros, and therefore perhaps the Pope will also like you when you give him your rhinoceros.

You no longer have a rhinoceros. They eat a lot.

Your elephant can relax a little.

Against

You no longer have a rhinoceros.

You might never again get the opportunity to learn who would win in a fight between the elephant and the rhinoceros.

The Wreck of the Rhino

Within four months of arriving in Lisbon the king was already planning to send Ganda away. The white elephant had been such a hit with the Medici pope the previous year that King Manuel thought to replicate its success by sending this even scarcer giant for the papal menagerie.

Pope Leo X loved his elephant.

Ganda was to be sent later that same year, in December 1515, along with other gifts from the East – two wooden kegs, two jugs, two water bowls for hand washing, two ewers, and six golden cups – as well as a gilded iron chain to bind Ganda and a green velvet collar decorated with roses and a fringe.

Ganda's feet were chained for the journey, and it was this, according to Paolo Giovio, that caused the rhinoceros's death.

...

In 1516 the new young ruler of France, King Francis I, would invite an ageing Leonardo da Vinci to live and work in the Loire Valley and Leonardo would take with him his most famous work of all – the little painting hanging in the Louvre, known as 'Mona Lisa'.

Cardinal Luigi of Aragon loved to travel and on one of his adventures he took Antonio de Beatis, canon of Molfetta and Luigi's chaplain, to document the trip. It was Antonio who noted Leonardo's description of the painting, as well as Leonardo's remark that the painting had been commissioned by Pope Leo X's brother, Giuliano de Medici.

Although they had been on opposite sides of the Battle of Marignano the previous year (which Francis had won) the French king and the Medici pope had similar tastes and when Francis learned that a rhinoceros was going to be sailing past Marseilles on its way to Rome just when he was visiting, he had to go and see it. So, in January 1516, with the Portuguese ship anchored at the island of If off the Marseilles coast,[14] Ganda was unloaded, much to the delight of the king and queen.

...

It should not have been a long journey from Marseilles to Rome, along the Alpine Côte d'Azur and Ligurian Riviera, but at the end of January or the beginning of February they were surprised by a storm a short way off Porto Venere. The ship was lost.

Paolo Giovio best describes the wreck:

But Neptune grudged Italy this beast of unusual ferocity, which ought to have been put to an amazing contest with an elephant on the sand of the amphitheatre. Neptune snatched it away when the vessel on which it was being transported ran aground on the cliffs of Liguria and sank in a storm that it

---

14   Da Costa, whose account of Ganda is generally the most forensic, mentions in a footnote that the Marseilles island would have been either Pomegues or Ratoneau, being the two largest. The island of If (also famous for being the setting for the imprisonment of Dumas's Count of Monte-cristo), however, makes a strong claim for itself and today sells t-shirts of Dürer's Ganda in the island shop.

could not deal with. Sorrow was universal, all the more so in that the beast was accustomed to swim across the Ganges and the Indus, the deepest rivers of its native land. It was believed that it could have swum to the shore above the Porto Venere, even though the rocks were high and very rugged, if it had not been shackled with huge chains and, its proud attempt to escape not succeeding, it had not yielded to the god of the sea.[15]

It's a shame the rhinoceros died, he says, because Ganda should have been fighting another elephant in Rome.

...

This stretch of the sea and coast is a protected wildlife conservation area, with Cuvier's beaked whales, sperm whales, pilot whales and a range of dolphins. In the sea off Portofino there is a submerged bronze statue, the 'Christ of the Abyss', with arms outstretched as though readying to catch something.

...

---

15   Translated from Giovio's 1554 *Elogia virorum bellica virtute illustrium* by Jonathan Trench.

Even Neptune did not want to keep the rhinoceros. Ganda's body is said to have washed up on a beach, where it was dragged ashore, stuffed and sent on to Rome.[16]

---

16   Deep breath. The popular story if you search through the internet, or if you read the best twentieth century accounts of the Ganda (those written by Bedini or Lach or Pimentel) state that Ganda was washed up on the French coast at Villefranche, back near Cannes. Donald Lach is one of the historians to make this claim in his *Asia in the Making of Europe*. Lach writes that the stuffed rhino arrived in Rome in February 1516, adding that this was 8 months after the elephant Hanno's death. But King Manuel wrote to his ambassador in Rome in August 1516 to say that he was only just made aware of the loss of the ship. And more than this, Hanno did not die until June 1516. Lach cites da Costa and Matos as his two sources for this information, but neither da Costa nor Luis Matos mentions Villefranche.

It seems likely that Lach simply meant to write 1517 rather than 1516 and was repeating some of the errors in dating made by earlier chroniclers like Damião de Góis. But even imagining this was the case the Villefranche detail seems questionable. Manuel claims to be uncertain of the loss of Ganda in August. Even though this is likely a lie, Manuel would not have told such a lie to his ambassador in Rome if in fact it was common knowledge that he was in the process of stuffing Ganda in Lisbon. So we can probably assume that even by August 1516 the body had not made its way back to Lisbon. This being the case, either Ganda was many months – including several summer months – at sea floating, sinking, decaying, being nibbled by lampreys and sharks before washing up mangled on the Côte d'Azur, or... this didn't happen at all.

In the two sources most contemporary to the wreck – Giovio and Gois – it is suggested that Ganda washed up closer to the wreck itself. Giovio has this near to Portovenere, while Gois has it off the coast of Genoa. Taken at their vaguest, both could be accurate.

This, then, seems much more plausible: Ganda died on the Ligurian coast, was washed up drowned and still shackled, stuffed and taken to the Pope from there.

a strange bloated fish

sinking like a saturated woodlouse in a forgotten bucket

unique certainly, but by far the least impressive porpoise

I.

'On what are we to base the likeness for this bloated, mangled thing?' asked the taxidermist.

'I might be able to find you a sketch,' his assistant replied.

The taxidermist thought a moment. 'No,' he said. 'Fetch me the poem.'

'Yes sir. Anything else?'

'We're going to need more straw.'

II.

Ganda stood
a likeness
of a likeness

in gilded shackles

III.

The hedgehog discarded the stalks
of the vines in his allegory

but this
story
is nothing
but stalks

Appendix: an encounter with the Indian Rhinoceros

While

    in a

        rural

            part of

                Nepal

                    I went

                        on one of those

                            guided walks

                                the travel books

                                    warn you about.

                            We got up early

                      and wandered

                  into the jungle

              with two guides,

          one carrying a

      stout, flexible

bamboo cane.

    The guide

        spotted her first.

        We were on

            the edge of

                the tree line,

                    on foot, following

                      a path along a

low mud bank,

on the other

side of which

stood a field

of tall grass.

That's where we saw her, for just a second: the Indian rhinoceros.

She disappeared

into the tall

grass, but as

we continued

along the mud

bank she would

pop out from

the grass now

and then, always

safely on the other

side. Until, that is,

the bank ended. We

found ourselves

on a path that

cut through the

jungle and the mud

bank and into the field,

and so did the rhinoceros.

She turned her head.

The guide said, 'Stand

still.' Then she turned

her whole body

to face us

on the path.

At this point,
I recalled
having read
something
about running
away in zigzags
because rhinoceroses
can't turn very well.
I also recalled the
traveller tale that
it's not only the horn
you have to worry about
but the rhino's tongue,
which is like sand
paper and can tear
off your skin with
a single lick.
A traveller I met
said he knew someone
who had seen it
happen.
But I trusted
the guides. I
would follow their lead.
They must have done this
a hundred times before.

They were,

naturally,

very quiet, not

wishing to startle

the rhinoceros,

so I looked

round. They

were gone. They

had run away

(zigzagging?

I'll never know)

and hidden

behind

the trees.

Bibliography

Albuquerque, Bras de, (trans. Walter de Gray Birch), *The Commentarues of the Great Afonso Dalboquerque*, London: Hakluyt Society, 1884.

Bahadur, Khan, *A History of Gujarat*, Bombay: Longmans, Green & Co., 1938.

Bedini, Silvio A., *The Pope's Elephant*, London: Penguin, 1997.

Browne, Thomas, *Pseudodoxia Epidemica*, London, 1650.

Brunhoff, Jean de, *The Babar Collection*, London: Egmont, 2016.

Buddhist Scriptures, London: Penguin Books, 2004.

Da Costa, A. Fontoura, *Deambulations of the Rhinoceros (Ganda) of Muzafar, King of Cambay, from 1514 to 1516*, Lisbon, 1937.

Clarke, TH, *The Rhinoceros from Durer to Stubbs*, London: Philip Wilson, 1988.

Fontoura da Costa, A. *Les Deambulations du Rhinoceros de Modofar, Roi de Camba ye, de 1514 a 1516*, Lisbon, 1937.

Giovio, Paulo (trans. Jonathan Trench), *Elogia virorum bellica virtute illustrium*, 2019.

Ionesco, Eugene (trans. Donald Watson), *Rhinoceros / The Chairs / The Lesson*, London: Penguin, 1962.

Indikopleustes, Kosmas (trans. J.W. McCrindle), in *Ancient India as Described by Ktêsias the Knidian*, London, Trübner & Co, 1882.

Isidore of Seville (trans. Stephen A. Barney, W.J. Lewis, J.A. Beach, Oliver Berghof), *Etymologies*, Cambridge: Cambridge University Press, 2011.

Lach, Donald, *Asia in the Making of Europe*, University of Chicago Press, 1994.

Lloyd, Joan Barclay, *African Animals in Renaissance Literature and Art*, OUP, 1971.

Mandeville, Sir John (trans. C.W.R.D. Moseley). *The Travels of Sir John Mandeville*, Penguin, 2005.

'Number 75: Durer's Rhinoceros', in *A History of the World in 100 Objects.*, BBC Radio 4, 2010.

McCrindle, J. W. *Ancient India as Described by Ktêsias the Knidian*, London: Trübner & Co, 1882.

Merton, Thomas, *Raids on the Unspeakable*, New York: New Directions, 1966.

Norman, K.R., *The Rhinoceros Horn*, Oxford: Pali Text Society, 1984.

Passarello, *Animals Strike Curious Poses*, New York: Sarabande, 2017.

Penni, Giovanni Giacomo (trans Sophy Downes), Forma & Natura & Costumi de lo Rinocerothe stato condutto importogallo dal Capitanio de larmata del Re & altre belle cose condutte dalle insule nouamente trouate', 2019.

Physiologus (trans. Michael J. Curley), Chicago: University of Chicago Press, 2009.

Pliny the Elder (trans. Philemon Holland). *Natural History*, London, 1601.

Sachau, Edward C. (trans.), *Alberuni's India*, London: Paul Trench, Trübner & Co., 1910.

Vasari, Giorgio (trans. Kenneth Gouwens), *Lives of the Artists*, Massachusetts: Harvard University Press, 2013.

Vaughan, Herbert, *The Medici Popes*, London: Methuen, 1908.
White, TH (trans.), *The Book of Beasts*, New York: Dover Publications, 1984.

Yang, Shou-zhong (trans.) *The Divine Farmer's Materia Medica*, Colorado: Blue Poppy press, 1998.

Acknowledgements

Gratitude is owed to a few people who have helped in various ways with the construction of this rhinoceros, most urgent thanks being owed to Sophy Downes and Charlie Sherratt. Sophy Downes made the translations in the 'Penni Dreadful' chapter, managing to capture both the fun and the cringeworthy aspects of the original Italian poem. (Thank you to Rose Ferraby for putting us in touch.) Charlie Sherratt created the illustrations in 'Dürer's Rhinoceros' after images by Albrecht Dürer, Hans Burgmair, and the artist who made the lovely little woodcut for Penni's publication.

Further thanks are owed to Jonathan Trench for his translation of Giovio, which appears in 'The Wreck of the Rhino', and also to Annemarie Jordan Gschwend and Kees Rookmaaker for trying to help me unravel some knots in the original sources.

LAY OUT YOUR UNREST